Hallowe'en

Mary O'Keeffe

G GILL EDUCATION

We do not have school when it is **Hallowe'en**. We have lots of fun when it is **Hallowe'en**!

I do not like it when it is dark.

The lamps come on when it gets dark. I like it when the lamps are lit.

There are a lot of **witches** at **Hallowe'en**. A **witch** has a **spell book**. It is big.

A witch's wand can be made from any material, but it is usually made from wood. Ash, oak and willow wands are very powerful!

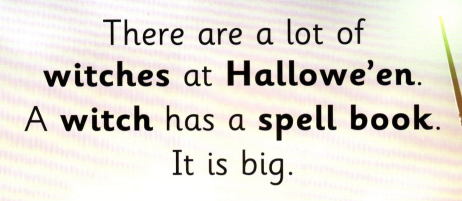

It is full of dust!
It has a lot of spells.
You have to be the best
witch to cast a spell!

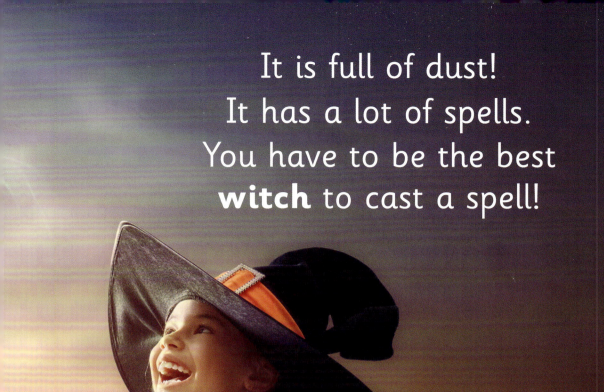

You have to get a big pot.

When it gets hot, you put lots of bits and bobs in the pot.

Give it a mix!

You put your hands up and cast the spell.

Zip, zap, zell!

I can cast a spell!

A **witch** has a cat. The cat sits on her lap. The cat is dark.

The cat can help the **witch**. She can get frogs, bats and socks for the **witch's** spells!

Most witches have black cats!

Most pets do not like **Hallowe'en**.
They do not like the big bangs.
They can get a bit sad
when it is **Hallowe'en**.

It is better to let your dog or cat come in when it gets dark. Give them a hug and a big pet. Be kind to your pet at **Hallowe'en**.

I like to have barmbrack at **Hallowe'en**.
Yum, yum!

Barmbrack is a sweet bread speckled with raisins. It is delicious toasted!

Mam cuts some and puts butter on it. If you get the ring, you will get lots of luck!

Hallowe'en is here for all of us!
Let's go and dress up!
We will have fun!